# They Were the Shoes of ALL Shoes

# They Were the Shoes of ALL Shoes

Written by Alva James

Illustrated by Crystal L. Caraway

Xulon Press
2301 Lucien Way #415
Maitland, FL 32751
407.339.4217
www.xulonpress.com

ISBN-13: 978-1-54567-934-0

# This book is dedicated ....

To every child who will get to hear this story, whether you read it yourself or it's read to you by your parent or guardian. To every child who will lay his head on a pillow at night to go to sleep, wondering if they will ever be special enough to fit into the "popular crowd." To the little girls and boys who feel awkward as you pull the covers over your head at night and read by flashlight because you prefer paper books rather than reading by a computer. To every child who falls asleep at night with that one thing on your mind that you hope by morning will happen, but you wake up and still have to wait.

To every parent or guardian who will take the time to read this story to your child or any child in your care, or to make it available in your reading library. It is my desire to encourage you by saying the right fit matters, not for a moment, but for a lifetime! Your decisions today matter for their tomorrow. Measure them for destiny!

To my dear husband (Jacob) of 46 years and the father of our amazing four adult children who we together determined to measure for their future, even if we didn't get it all right. You were a real rock as we poured into them to prepare them for destiny. To my three beautiful grandchildren Kaia, Joshua and Jacob, may you always remember that just because it's popular it just might not be measured for you. Remember for a lifetime that your Bebe say's the right fit matters!

Lastly and especially, to my dear parents, Mr. and Mrs. Kelly and Margaret Monuel, who were known in our tiny little country community as "Mr. Kelly" and "Mrs. Margaret;" you took your role of parenting very seriously. I now appreciate you both more than I could've ever imagined for the depth of wisdom, faith, love and courage to parent me, not just for a moment, but to create a capacity in me for my destiny. Thanks for teaching me how to be a part of a community without losing sight of who I was created to be; and of how I fit into that community, not to be different but to make a difference.

**Thanks Daddy — I found the shoe that fits!**

They were the shoes of ALL shoes, or so Elaine thought. It seemed most of the girls in the school had a pair... at least the most popular girls, anyway.

Day in and day out it was all Elaine could think about at the time. They had to be the best shoes ever. This pair of shoes was much better looking than her black-and-white oxfords. Besides, all of the popular girls were wearing them.

As the clock on the wall in Mr. River's class ticked away, all Elaine could think about was getting home to make sure all of her chores were done in hopes that it would go well when her dad got home from work. She thought that she would ask him one more time about buying her a pair in hopes that this time he would say yes.

She was thinking how could she convince him this time of how really important it was for her to be like all of the rest of the popular girls in school. For sure, this time he would understand, or so she hoped.

Soon after the bell rang and she began rushing to gather her books to head home, Mr. Rivers asked if she was okay. He'd been watching her daydreaming during class.

"Yes sir!" she replied. "I just need to hurry home to do my chores before my dad gets home."

Mr. Rivers paused for a minute, smiled, and even looked a little puzzled, but said, "Good girl. I'll see you bright and early tomorrow." So off she went, hurrying home, walking ahead of her sisters to make sure her chores were done.

When she got home, her mother called out to her from the kitchen to ask her how her day at school had gone. "Aren't you going to come and eat your snack before you do your homework?" her mom asked.

Elaine didn't know exactly what to say. If she said she didn't want a snack she thought it might be rude. Her mom always took the time to make one for her and her sisters and sit with them as they ate after getting home each day.

Coming home each day was always a real treat, because she would smell dinner cooking, and many times there would be a cake or pie in the oven, too. Today was different though. Food was not on Elaine's list.

Elaine asked if she could be excused to go to her room to change her clothes and do her chores. Her mother smiled and slowly said, "Sure," while turning to check on whatever was baking in the oven.

Elaine hurried to her room to change her clothes, do her chores, and finish her homework before her dad got home. The evening went by so slowly, but she would make sure everything was done before her dad arrived.

er dad's coming home from work was always a highlight! It was always a big deal for her and her two sisters. It was always a race to see which one of them would get to him first. It usually would mean one would be on his shoulders, one in his arms and whoever was last to get to him usually would end up wrapped around one of his legs. He made coming home a happy time for them, often bringing home a special treat, but stopping to play and laugh with them. He would take the time to listen to how their day had gone before he went off to his room to change and bathe for dinner.

Certainly, today would be just like that, she hoped. Elaine sat wondering, after all of the rushing home to do her chores and homework, whether he would notice. Besides, she wanted to ask about the shoes before dinner.

Before dinner always seemed to be the best time, but today somehow seemed a bit different. Elaine was unsure by now if she should ask her dad again.

She thought to herself, "Maybe I've already asked too many times ..." Soon she heard the car door close and a moment later the back door being opened. For a second, she was slow in making her way to the door to greet her dad; it was one of the days she missed being picked up and ended up being the one hanging on to his leg. Even though she was late getting to him, he was late as well. He reached to put his lunch bucket down while being tackled by his three girls.

Even though he brought home his usual big smile, somehow today seemed very different to Elaine. She felt almost shy or nervous to ask her dad anything before or after dinner. She was always the one who never had a problem asking him for anything. Actually, her sisters would push her up to ask for things they were too shy to ask for, because she was the baby of the family. Somehow, they thought she would get a yes! "I need to find a way to ask quickly," she thought, "before he goes off to his room to shower and change for dinner."

Just then she heard her mom call out to them, "Dinner will be ready real soon, everybody wash your hands!" Elaine dashed to talk to her dad, but he quickly went off to get cleaned up and changed for dinner.

Elaine sat in the living room pondering once again, "Should I ask? What if he gets upset with me for asking again when he's already said no each time before?" Right then she heard her mother call again, so she hurried to the table and soon they were all sitting at the dinner table with their dad saying grace.

They all began to eat and enjoy what her mom had cooked that day and with each swallow it seemed the words were stuck in her throat. Certainly, she would never be able to ask again, she thought.

You see, Elaine was old enough to know if her dad ever said no, there was a real reason and his no really meant no!

After dinner was over, she made sure her dad saw her helping her mom and sisters clear the table so one of her sisters could wash the dishes. He looked over with a smile and went to sit in his relaxing chair in the living room. Elaine walked back and forth, wondering if she should dare ask again.

One thing for sure she knew was that her dad and mom always agreed about their decisions and there was no reason to even ask her mom. Besides, they'd always made a BIG deal about shoes. She wondered why, when they talked about choosing shoes, they called them "foundations." It was strange to her. "What on earth is a foundation? I thought they were shoes," she would think to herself. Her dad would say, "Make sure that baby's got a good foundation."

5

Elaine wondered why her father had such a love for shoes, and why they were so important to him, until one day her mother sat her and her sisters down to tell them the story of how their dad grew up.

She explained to them that their father had grown up very poor. His mom had died when he was very young, about four years old, and even as a little boy he started working to help his father. His father often didn't have enough to buy shoes for him and his growing brothers and sisters. His feet grew really fast and he would always grow out of his shoes before he would get a new pair. Many times he had to wear hand-me-downs, shoes that were busted or with holes in the bottom. Many times he had to walk for miles on his bare feet, even to school.

She told them about the day he got his first real pair of shoes. Those shoes were really special to him and he took great care of them. He would clean them every evening after he took them off and tuck them neatly under his bed at night.

Then one day, after another growth spurt, the bottoms were gone and the toe came apart. It was a sad day for him as a young boy. Even though the shoes looked good for a long time, what he forgot was that his feet were still growing very fast. Another thing he didn't really realize was that no matter how nice the shoe looked on the outside, his feet still needed room to grow and develop.

Somehow that explained why Elaine's parents always took her and her sisters to this special store when they would go into town to shop for shoes.

The special store was Bob's Shoe Store. They called the owner "Mr. Bob." Mr. Bob was a really nice Jewish man and he ran the store along with his wife. They both were very kind to Elaine's dad and mom. She would come from the back and give the biggest greetings whenever they entered the store, and take the time to sit with her parents to talk about how the feet of their girls were growing and developing.

One thing Elaine always noticed, though, was Mr. Bob's shoes were not always the coolest looking shoes around. His shoes were not like Butler's or Baker's shoe store. Mr. Bob's shoes looked more like shoes her dad or mom would wear, she often thought. They looked really plain, but really comfortable.

The other two stores were where most of the kids, teens, and their parents always shopped for shoes.

Those shoes were more popular, it seemed but her parents insisted on shopping at Mr. Bob's for whatever reason. One reason, for sure, was that Elaine's sister, Lavern, always needed a "better made" shoe because she was a lot rougher on shoes, they said. So, that meant Bob's Shoe Store was the place to go.

Each time they visited Mr. Bob's store he would insist on measuring her and her sister's feet. He would sit on a stool that had a metal foot measurer and show her dad and mom just how much their feet had grown, and suggest the right size for them to buy. He would show them just how much room was safe to keep them from tripping, but also he wanted to make sure their feet would have just the right amount of support, as their feet were growing and developing. The other fancy shoe stores were always overrun with people.

t seemed like they were much busier than Mr. Bob's store.

She felt odd at times watching a lot of her friends and other families across the street shopping for shoes. Elaine felt like she was somehow missing out on something. There were a few times when her father would walk them across the street to look at all of the other shoe stores, even sometimes buy them a pair, but one thing she always noticed was that there were a lot of young sales people walking around.

The place would always be buzzing with laughter and ringing of the cash register. There was not a lot of discussion about what was best for the children's feet. They were making a lot of money selling shoes, though. The kids would be excited to get exactly what they wanted, and the parents always seemed in a hurry to get out of the store.

Elaine would often wonder what was different. Why was there so much fuss being made about their feet? Besides, wasn't it just about finding the best-looking shoe, trying it on, and buying it?

There were a few times when Elaine's father would allow her and her sisters to choose shoes from those fancy stores, but never without visiting Mr. Bob first. Somehow, she noticed those shoes didn't quite fit as well, or last as long, as Mr. Bob's shoes.

Well, this particular day had finally come and Elaine had made up her mind to ask her father just one more time about the brown-and-tan oxford shoes. They were just a bit fancier than the black-and-white oxford at Mr. Bob's store, right? Praying he would say yes, somehow deep down she had felt he for sure would say no and give her a big discussion about why he didn't think it was a good idea. To her surprise she asked one more time – and of all things, this time he said Yes!

Wow, did she hear right. she thought? Did her dad really actually say yes to the shoe this time?

Elaine had gone all those months watching most of the girls at her school wearing this shoe, even her friends, and her dad had insisted on saying no. Her father called her mom into the living room and said, "Get the girls ready early in the morning. We'll be going into town to Baker's shoe store to get Elaine the shoes she wants."

Her mom paused for a minute, smiled, and said slowly, "Okay girls, time to bathe and brush your teeth, we have an early day tomorrow."

Going to sleep that night was really hard for Elaine. All she could do was think about finally having those shoes on her feet. She would finally be in style and included with the popular girls. She would not be so different anymore. Finally, she fell off to sleep, and soon before she knew it she heard her mom calling, "Rise and shine, it's time to get up and get ready to go into town!"

She smelled breakfast cooking, so her feet hit the floor and she hurried to get dressed. Soon they were done eating and in the car headed into town. She was shocked and excited at the same time. She was so thrilled that she had finally convinced her father to buy the shoes she'd wanted for so long.

It was 13 miles into the city and she thought it would be just like any other day in the car with laughing, singing, and lots of talking with her family, but this day was very different. Today was really quiet in the car. There was so singing, just a little bit of chatter, but no singing.

"Oh no!" she thought. "Is this a trip to town with no laughing, singing or much talking? Does this mean we won't visit our regular In 'n' Out Burger on the way home?" she pondered. You see, it was always a highlight for their family to visit their famous In 'n' Out Burger or the Whataburger on the way home when they would drive into town. She didn't want anything to mess up the usual plan, but she certainly didn't want to say anything. The ride seemed longer than any other day they had driven into town.

Finally, they arrived in town. Her father parked across the street from the courthouse that sat right in the middle of their town square. He got out and put money into the parking meter. Elaine peered through the window to try to see if he looked happy or not. She watched him as he walked back to the car. He leaned his head into the car and said, "Ok, let's go!"

Sure enough, off they all walked. "Hold on…" she thought, "he's headed to Mr. Bob's. I thought he'd said yes to the other store and to getting that other shoe?"

She sighed with deep disappointment when they entered the store; it was their regular routine to get their feet measured and wait as her father talked to Mr. Bob. They spoke very quietly, but soon and to her surprise she heard her dad say, "Okay, thank you, Sir!"

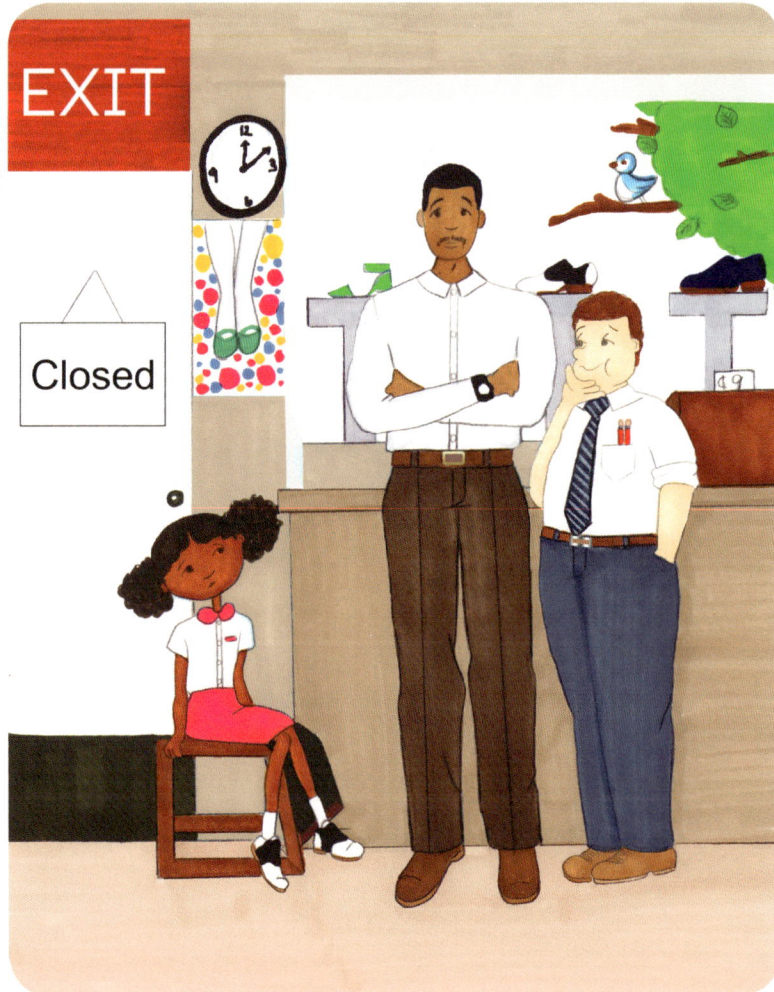

Elaine thought to herself, 'We're leaving? No shoes?' when all of a sudden her dad took her by the hand to walk her across the road toward Baker's shoe store.

"Am I dreaming?" she thought. "Could it really be true?" Well it was true, and she was so excited. "Finally!" she thought to herself.

When they entered the store, one of the young sales people was right there to ask if he could help. Her dad said, "Sure can," then told Elaine to show the sales guy the shoe she wanted.

With a big smile she walked over and picked up the shoe and handed it to the salesman.

Off to the back he rushed. "Did he forget to measure my feet?" she thought, but soon he returned to ask what size. "Hmmm..." Elaine pondered. "No measuring? No discussion?" Her dad told him the size, because even if they decided to shop in another store, Mr. Bob would always advise them of just the right size to buy.

They sat down to wait for the salesman, her heart beating with excitement. Soon the salesman showed up with the box. She was so excited; she could hardly wait to try them on.

When he opened the box, even the smell of them made her smile; they were a beautiful suede material. The shoe felt really nice, too. The sales guy sat to help her put the shoe on and all of a sudden, the moment had arrived. The shoes she had waited for were now on her feet and suddenly she discovered what would have to be a secret.

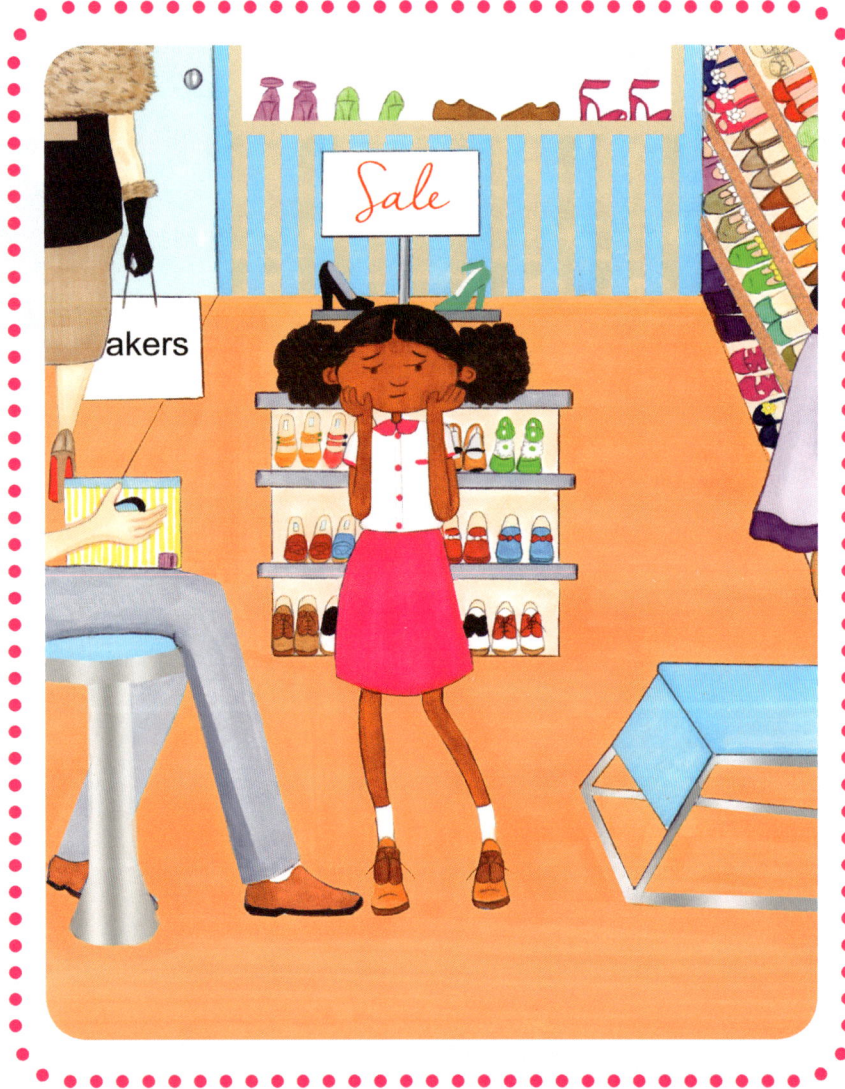

What Elaine discovered was that this shoe didn't fit her! Oh no, it was the right size, alright. Heaven forbid, her dad had visited Mr. Bob first as always, so the size was right; that wasn't the problem. What Elaine discovered was that after all of the dreaming, asking, and waiting for that shoe, she now discovered that shoe didn't fit her. She didn't even like the shoe on her, how it looked, or even felt.

This was something that she couldn't dare say to her dad, especially after all of those months of asking for this shoe and driving 13 miles to the store. For sure she couldn't say anything because without a doubt it would mess up their usual lunch visit, and most likely upset everyone else, too.

How could she tell her dad that? With all the trouble he had gone through to make sure she got those shoes... even changing his no to a yes. Soon she heard the sales guy ask, "How do you like them?"

Elaine didn't utter a word and just smiled. Her dad said, "Just tie them up, she'll be wearing them home!" The sales guy was so excited because he'd just made a quick sale, but Elaine wasn't happy at all. "What!" She thought. Wearing them home? What happened? Wasn't she supposed to be happy? After all, she got what she wanted, right?

As soon as they were tied up, her dad stood at the counter to pay for them.

As she watched the sales guy put her old shoes in the box and soon in a bag, she thought, "Oh my, all this time?" She thought to look up at her dad, and somehow at that moment he almost seemed like he was smiling.

She made sure to say thank you to her father and off they went to their famous lunch stop, and soon on the road back home.

Interesting enough, it was that same kind of quiet in the car on the way home, at least for Elaine. Her sisters were laughing and playing, her dad and mom were talking about the next week, but she had finally figured out something that her dad most likely knew all along.

Soon they were pulling up to the house. She hurried out of the car and off to her room she went to find just the right outfit to wear with her shoes the next time she went to school. After many changes she finally found what she thought would be perfect. Soon the call came for supper. At the table everyone was talking and laughing, but all Elaine could think about was what the girls would say when she arrived at school with her new shoes.

It started to get late, and when she was done and finally in bed that night, all she could think about was all of the times she'd asked her dad and mom for those shoes, and dreamed of how she would look in them. She'd thought about how all of her friends would react seeing her in those shoes, but now that her parents had finally agreed, she now discovered that they didn't even fit her. She really didn't like them, especially on her, but now she would just have to pretend she really liked the shoe.

Monday came and it was time to go to school. Her mother called her to make sure she would get up to be ready on time for her dad to drive her and her sisters to school that morning. When breakfast was done, she gathered her books and hurried to kiss her mom goodbye. Her mom stood in the door and watched them drive off. Elaine waved back, and thought, "This is the day that I will finally fit in."

Soon they arrived at the school and Elaine saw her principal, Mr. Mack, standing there talking to some of her friends before the bell rang. Before Elaine got out of the car, she had hoped that all of the popular girls would be standing around to see that she had finally got "the shoes" and just as she hoped, they were all standing there, but as she started to get out of the car, the first thing she noticed was that a new shoe had popped up.

"What?" she thought to herself, "You mean after all this time of waiting and now another shoe? Plus, I'm wearing the shoes that I don't even like anymore? You mean they are starting to wear something else? Oh No! Not now. Just as soon as I get this pair, there is another pair? You mean I'm the 'odd girl' again?"

Her dad slowed leaving the school while waving goodbye. He said to her, "I hope you have a really good day at school." He had said that many times, but today seemed just a bit different.

And that is when it suddenly dawned on her, that her dad had chosen that moment to agree to buy that shoe to teach her a big and much needed lesson.

She later found out that her dad had always known that that shoe didn't fit her, but he wanted Elaine to discover that on her own. You see, he'd said no so many times to spare her, but realized that there would be some lessons she would have to learn even if they were lessons like this one.

He wanted her to discover that every shoe, no matter what it looks like and how it fits someone else, may not always fit you. He wanted her to realize that everything was not meant for her and that she should learn how to celebrate her own special style.

Her mom always said to her, "What if someone is watching you and thinks you're special? What if someone thinks that they want to be like you, while you're trying to be like everyone else?"

To Elaine's surprise, many years later after she had grown up and become a young lady, she saw one of the popular girls from her old school. The girl told her how much she'd observed and admired her all through school. She observed how her dad and mom took time with her and her sisters. She and so many of her friends had admired how she and her sisters stood out among the crowd rather than always trying to fit in.

Elaine thought, "Are you serious?" Fitting in was the biggest thing for her up until the day her dad taught her the lesson of a lifetime... a lesson she would never ever forget. It was a really important lesson that she, too, would one day pass on to her children and grandchildren.

That day years ago at her school, she learned that it's okay to be different! It's ok to stand out! It's okay not to always want to fit in. Most of all, be yourself: Never force yourself to fit into anything that doesn't fit you, no matter who else is wearing it.

# Acknowledgement

This book is the first of three initial stories I am excited to share, filled with life lessons from my childhood. It's my way of saying thank you for the unforgettable experiences and people who were vital in shaping and forming me into an adult. Writing about them, and what they taught me, is more rewarding than I could have ever imagined.

A very special thanks to Nola Boea, who came alongside to serve this vision at the very inception of Relay Media Group. You have been a constant encouragement. Your brilliance, work ethic, wisdom and foresight is amazing! Your consistent support has been unwavering!

I'm forever grateful to my friend Donna Scuderi, a major editor and writer who took the time to read the rough draft of this story several years ago, smiled, and nudged me on to share my experiences through writing. You have no idea of how much it meant to me. I love you.

Thank you to Dr. Mark Chironna, one of the busiest pastors and bishops I know, who said to me publicly, "Alva I read [the synopsis] you wrote, and it is in your DNA ...run with it!" Both you and Lady Ruth continue to encourage me, and so many others, to be intentional as we spread our wings and look boldly to the future with great expectation!

To one of my dearest sister-friends, Anita Howard, who continues to stand with me in spite of many delays along the way. Your voice on the phone encouraged me during many intense challenges, saying, "I love you! You've got this! I'm praying for you!" Just knowing you were yet standing with me no matter what was heartfelt!

Thank you especially to my dear husband Jacob who is readily there as a constant encouragement, and to help me think through many ideas relating to my way of expressing "country talk." You are an authentic farm boy; your honest and "cut to the chase" feedback is forever your signature.

Thank you to my grown children, Oran, Africa, Areisha and Gabrielle. I'm sure you've heard these stories more than once or twice, yet you consistently support the passion in my heart to pass them on. Thanks for the love, encouragement, gifts and surprises, and teases about checks in the mail, to see this vision through.

Thanks to my three grandchildren, Kaia, Joshua, and Jacob, who listened vigorously to my reading of the rough draft of this story. I never told you who the author was until the story was over. The gleam in your eyes and delightful comments warmed my heart and said to me possibly other children would listen and catch what I wanted to pass on!

I want to thank God most of all, who placed me in a family with parents where the right shoes mattered more than what the crowd was wearing! I can never put a price on how valuable that lesson was and is to this day! Without you, I would have settled for the  wrong fit and possibly ended up with no story of value to pass on!

Thanks Daddy, Mama, and yes, Mr. Bob — that measuring made a difference! What a lesson found in shoes. They indeed were  the shoes of ALL shoes!

## About the Author

Alva was born into a small, closely knitted family in a small farm town. She gained much, wisdom and insight by observing the intentional and heartfelt sacrifice of her parents and an older generation. They sowed their lives as seed just as intently as they sowed seeds for harvest, as seasons yielded their fruitful increase that caused them to be nourished and to nourish their families and community year in and year out.

Years later, after being married for 46 years and fully embracing a season of parenting four children and now grandmother of three, she now finds it's time for her to share her life's stories. Alva was involved along the way in elementary education, music, stage productions, and youth and children's ministry for over 25 years. She traveled throughout North America and abroad for 20 years as a vocalist with an international music team. Her combined 40-plus years of gathered wisdom and experience throughout her journey in both the secular and Christian arena has brought her to a place of passionately passing her story on.

As a native Floridian and girl raised in the South, she speaks and writes from a truly down-home place that reaches the heart as she shares her real-life stories that have become gems and jewels for her to pass on to the next generation.

She founded Relay Media Group in 2011, where she shares the wit, wisdom and insight handed to her from her parents and those from her past, as gems and jewels to intentionally pass on to the next generation.

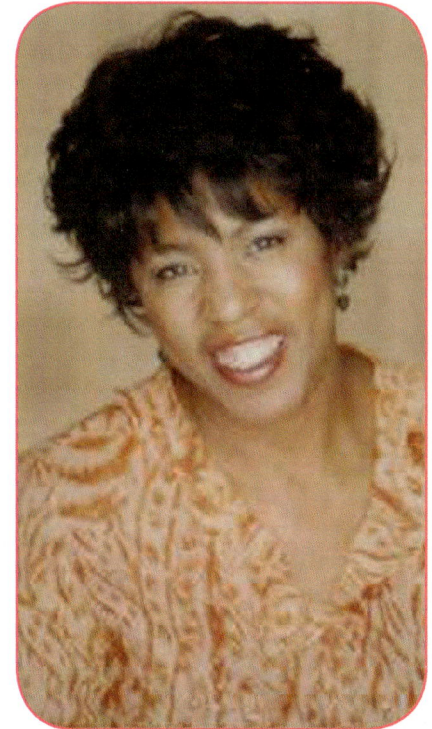

CPSIA information can be obtained at www.ICGtesting.com
Printed in the USA
LVIW011501271119
638723LV00008B/96

*9781545679340*